AVORITE PIANO SOLOS

LUE RIBBON ENCYCLOPEDIA

CONTENTS

BLUE RIBBON ENCYCLOPEDIA, Level One

AT THE TRADING POST, Louise Garrow
BEADED MOCCASINS, Bernice Frost
BOOGIE BRIGADE, Roger Grove
BROTHER RABBIT, Hazel Cobb
CALYPSO TUNE, Jon George
THE CELLO SINGS, Robert Schultz
DANCING BEARS, Robert Donahue
DAYDREAMS, William Gillock
DOO-DAD BOOGIE, David Carr Glover
DEUTSCHER TÄNZ, Jon George
FOLLOW ME, William Scher
THE GLASS CAROUSEL, Bruce Berr
GOBLIN'S DELIGHT, David Karp
GRANNY'S SERVING TEA, David Carr Glover
HOP SCOTCH, Bill Catania
THE ICE CREAM MAN, Robert Schultz
THE INDEX TWINS, Franz Mittler
IT'S A GAME, David Carr Glover
MARCH, Christine O'Neil
THE MILL WHEEL, June Weybright
MING LING, Mary Elizabeth Clark
MOON MARCH, Elvina Pearce
ORIENTAL LEGEND, Maryanne Nagy
THE OWL'S STORY, Marie Andrea
THE PLEASANT PEASANT, Jon George
PUPPET ON A STRING, David Karp
RAIN, RAIN, GO AWAY, Louis Sugarman
ROAMING, Hazel Cobb
SCOTCH HEATHER, M. Muettman
SIMPLE SOUL, Roger Grove
SNEAKY CREEPY THINGS, David Carr Glover
SPACE EXPLORER, John W. Schaum
SPANISH FEST, Elvina Pearce
TRICKY TRAFFIC, Louise Garrow
THE TRUMPET PLAYER, Hazel Cobb
TWO MARIONETTES, John Robert Poe
WALKIN' THE BASS, Marion Marwick
THE WICKED WITCH IS DEAD,
Carrie Flatau, David Carr Glover
WOODEN SHOES, Benjamin Wermel
YE OLDE FANFARE, Jon George

BLUE RIBBON ENCYCLOPEDIA, Level Three

ALLEGRO SPIRITOSO, Jon George
AN OLD VALENTINE, Earl Ricker
BITTERSWEET, Virginia Speiden Carper
BLACK CUBICALS, B.J. Rosco
BRAZILIANA, June Weybright
CASTANETTA, June Weybright
CIRCUS PARADE, David Carr Glover
COFFEE BEANS, Walter Noona
DREAM INTERLUDE, Mark Nevin
ESPAÑITA, Mark Nevin
FLAMENCO TIME, Emily Leitner Ervin

(Level Three, continued)

THE FLAMING TAMBOURINE, Walter Noona
GIVE THE BASSIST A BREAK, Robert Kelley
GLASS BELLS, Hazel Cobb
HAPPY, Condit Atkinson
HAPPY TIME, Roger Grove
HOPPING AND SKIPPING, Y. Gnessina
THE HUNTERS, David Carr Glover
INDIGO, Roger Grove
ISLAND SONG, Olive Nelson Russell
JAZZ MINIATURES, Mark Nevin
JO-JO THE JUGGLER, Everett Stevens
LUCKY SEVEN, Roger Grove
MILES OF BLUE, Tony Caramia
MORNING STAR, Sherman Storr
PERPETUAL MOTION, Hazel Cobb
REFLECTIONS OF THE MOON, Olive Dungan
ROCK 'N' ROLL BOOGIE, John W. Schaum
SMOOTH, Condit Atkinson
STRUTTIN', June Edison
TOCCATINA, Robert Schultz
VIVACE, Richard Faith
WALTZING TOGETHER, David Carr Glover

BLUE RIBBON ENCYCLOPEDIA, Level Four

BOOGIE EXPRESS, John W. Schaum
THE BOOGIE MAN, John W. Schaum
CANE AND SPATS, Samuel Spivak
CHILI-SAUCE, H.A. Fischler
COOL MULE, Marvin Kahn
CRAGGY GARDENS IN THE SPRING,
Sarah Louise Dittenhaver
DANCE OF THE WOODEN SHOES, Max Schuldt
ESCAPADE, Robert Schultz
FIREFLIES, Clara Jean Curzon
FLAMENCO, Mark Nevin
GIGA, Gian-Carlo Menotti
GYPSY CAMPFIRE, Louis Sugarman
HOG RIVER RAG, James Carroll
INTRADA, June Weybright
JAZZ PRELUDE, Mark Nevin
LOTUS FLOWERS IN THE WIND, William Scher
MARCHE DE LA GARDE ROYALE, David Carr Glover
NOCTURNE, David Carr Glover
THE PEACOCK, Olive Dungan
PORTRAIT OF GERSHWIN, George Bermont
PRELUDE NO. 2, David Carr Glover
REFLECTIONS IN THE RAIN, Walter Noona
SCREEN DOOR RAG, Marjorie Burgess
SERENADE IN BLUE, Franz Mittler
SPANISH BLUES, Marvin Kahn
THE SPINNING TOP, George Anson
SUNDAY BEST, Dick Averre
WALTZ IN BLUE, Marvin Kahn
WINTER WIND, Gian-Carlo Menotti

THE KNIGHT'S TALE

JOHN ROBERT POE

3
2
2
poco
-
a
-
poco
4
1
3
1
rall
-
en
-
tan
-
do
mp
3
1
2
4
tempo primo
3
1

A BUTTERFLY FLUTTERS BY

JON GEORGE

Nimbly ♩. = 116

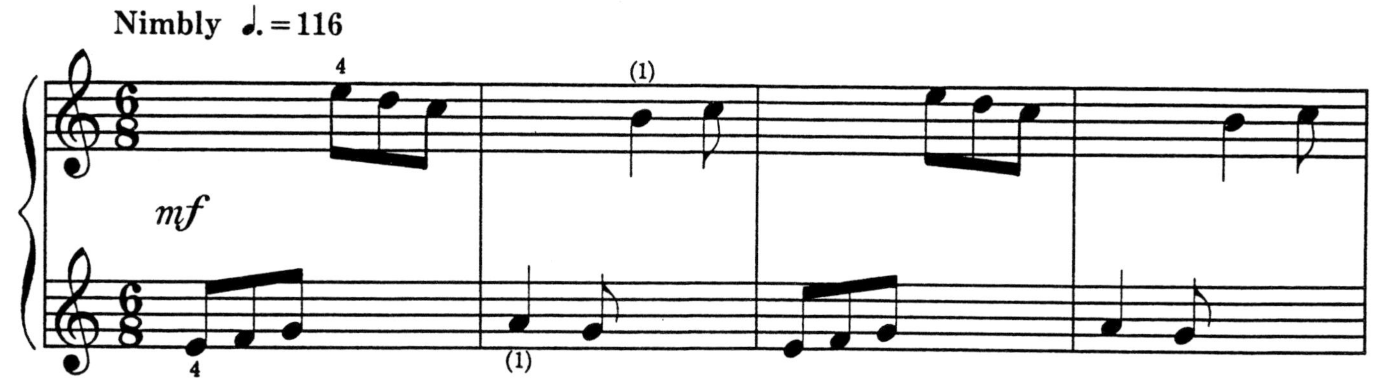

from Configurations 1B

THE MERRY-GO-ROUND

DAVID CARR GLOVER

f
cresc.
p
mf
rit.

DAYDREAMS

ROBERT SCHULTZ

Daydreams - 2 - 1

mp
mf
mp
p

To Ruth and Jack Luther

SAILORS SHINDIG

BENJAMIN WERMEL

Lively

mf

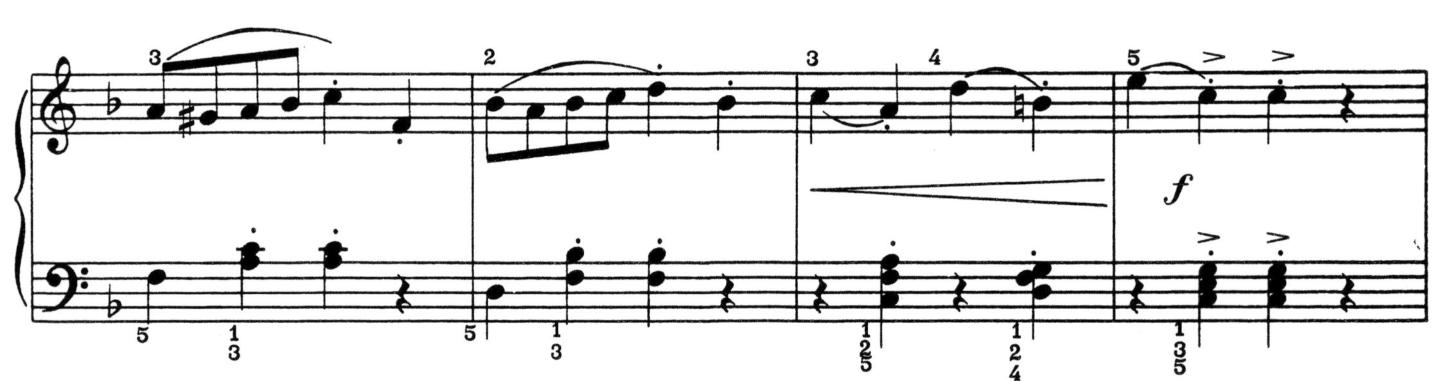

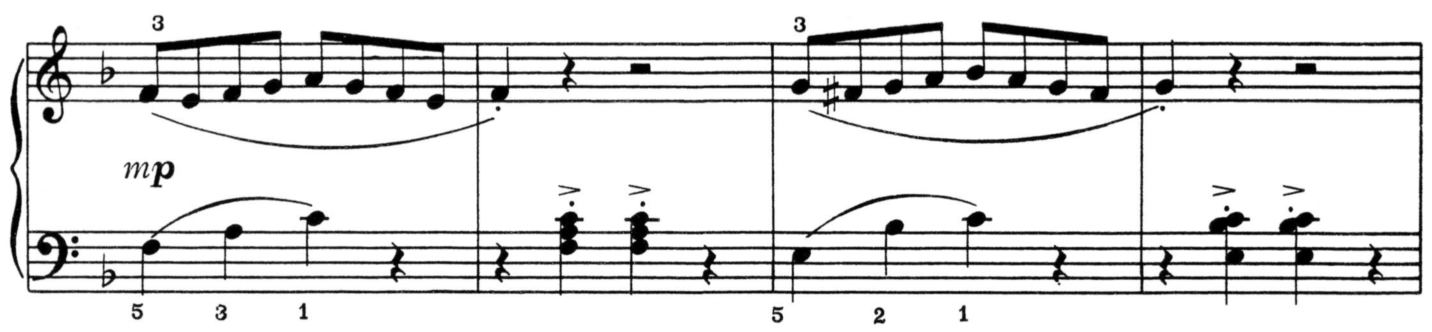

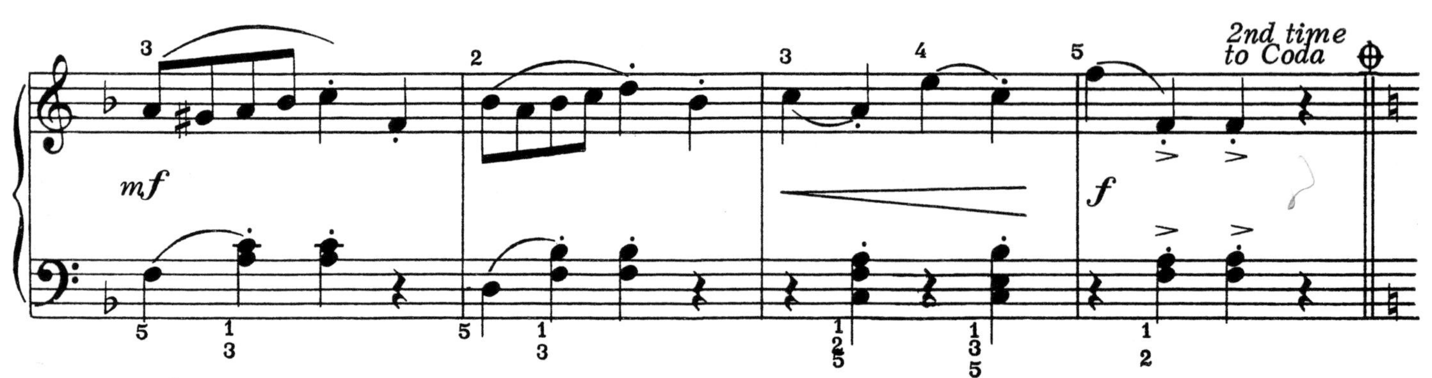

mp
mp
mf
mp
mp
mf
D.C. to Coda
f
Coda
p
f
ff

REFLECTIONS

ROBERT SCHULTZ

Gently, not too slow 𝅗𝅥 = 66-80

pp

espressivo

mp-p

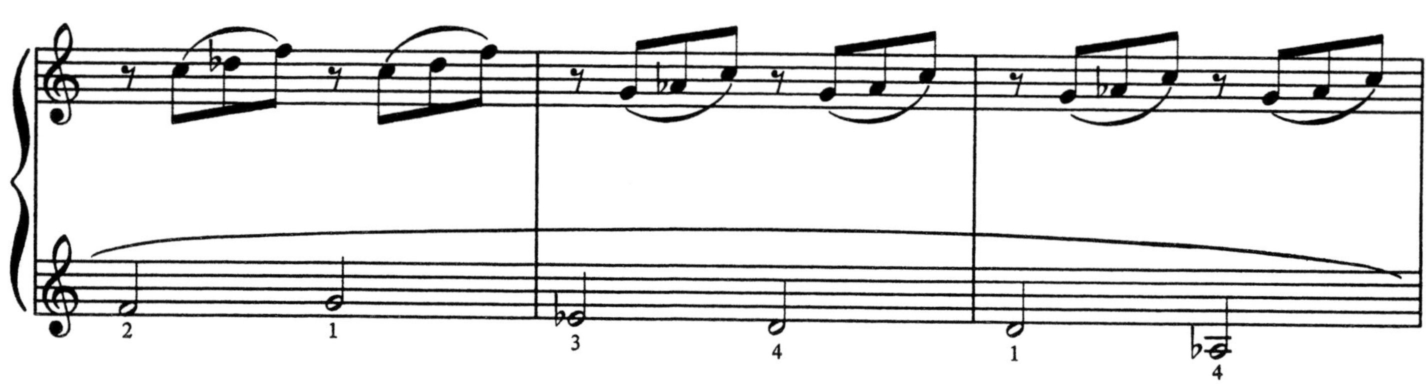

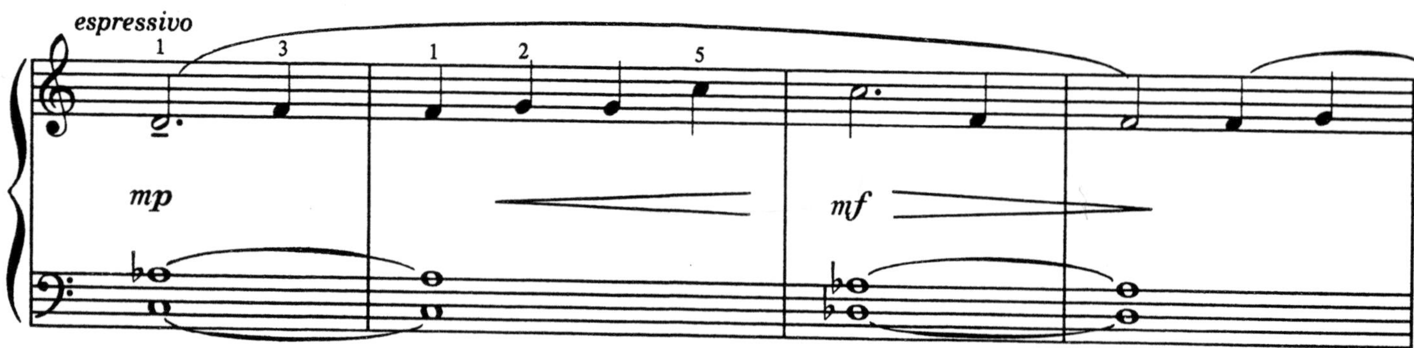

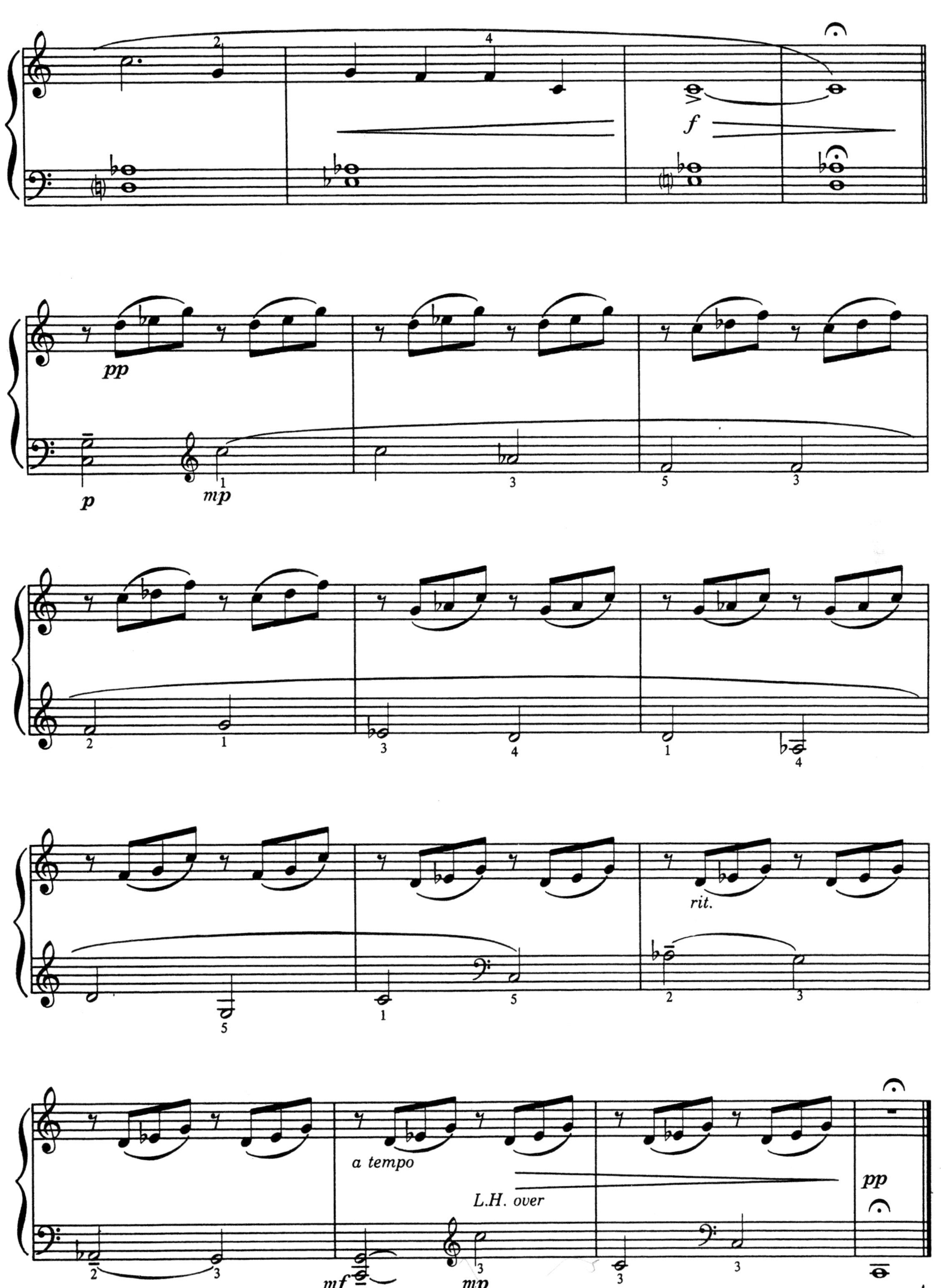
f
pp
p
mp
rit.
a tempo
L.H. over
mf
mp
pp

MELODY FOR A MONDAY MORNING

RALPH STEINER

from *Styles and Sounds*

A LA SONATINA

LOUISE CURCIO

THE VIKING

WALTER NOONA

ff
pp
ff
p
molto rit.
f
f
8va
l.h.
l.h.
sfz
ff

STROLL ON A WARM DAY

LYNN FREEMAN OLSON

8va
pp
8va
mp
holding back
pp
much slower
R.H.
L.H. over
ppp
8va
L.H. over

To David Nieves

DREAM OF THE TIN SOLDIER

WILLIAM SCHER

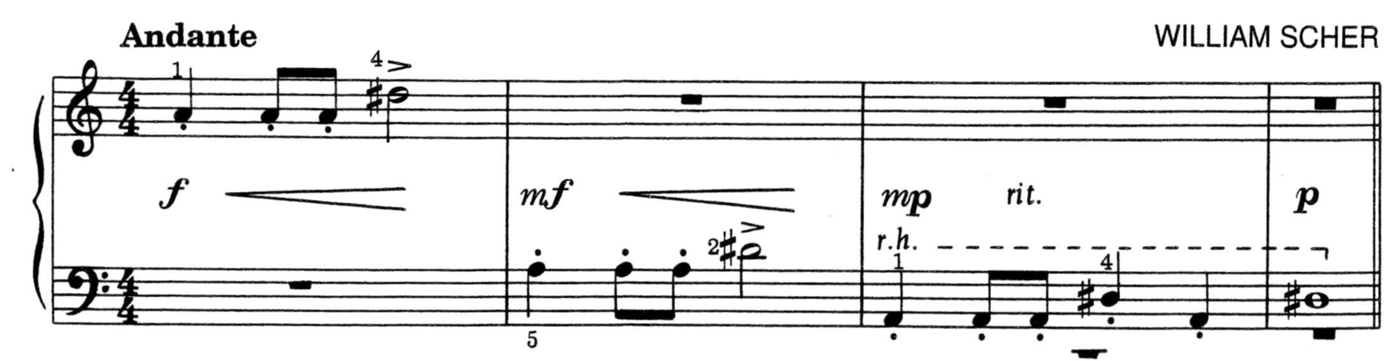

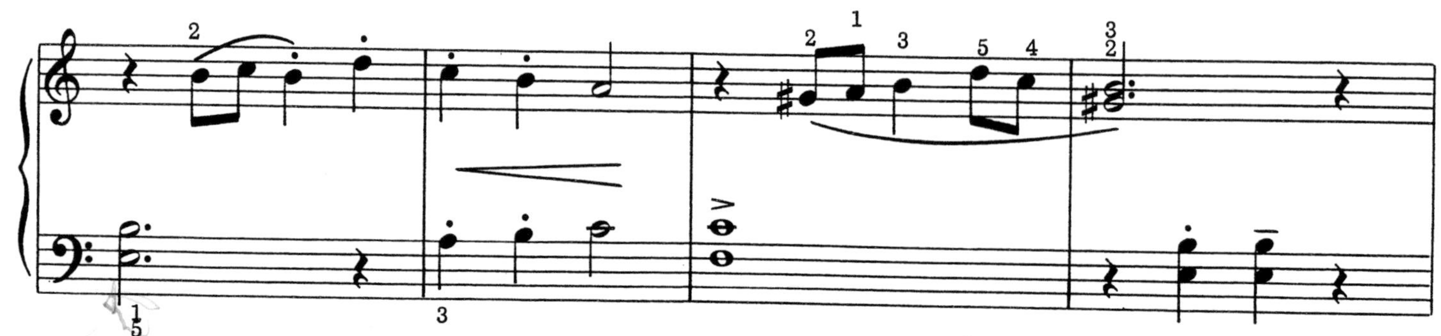

mf
rit.
a tempo
mf
ff
f
mf
r.h.
molto rit.
l.h.
Lento
p
poco dim.
rit.
pp

PICNIC TIME

MICHAEL BRODSKY

from Minute Melodies

R.H.
L.H.
R.H.
f
L.H.
R.H.
L.H.
R.H.
R.H.
L.H.
f
R.H.
L.H.
L.H.
mf
f

THE VILLAGE BAND

ROBERT DONAHUE

dim.
p
cresc.
f

CIRCUS CLOWNS

from *Sights to See*

ff
f
mf
p
mf
p
mp
mf
f

THE DARING COSSACK

WALTER NOONA

ff
ff
f

f
ff
cresc.
fff
sfz

BANJO TUNE

MICHAEL AARON

Happily

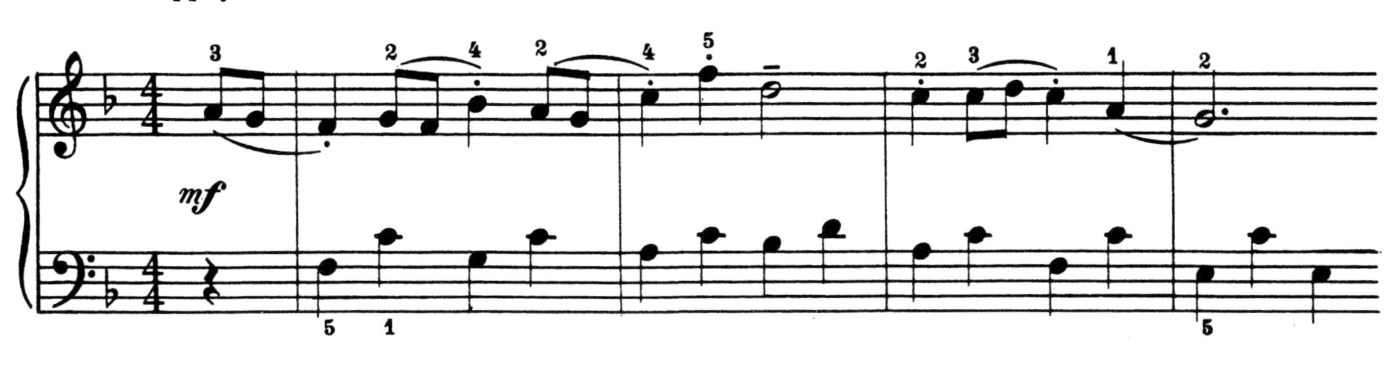

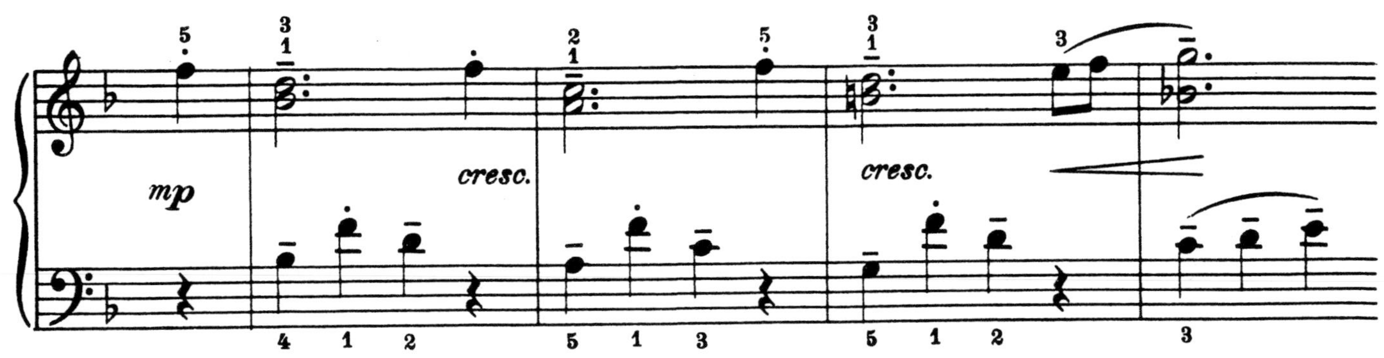

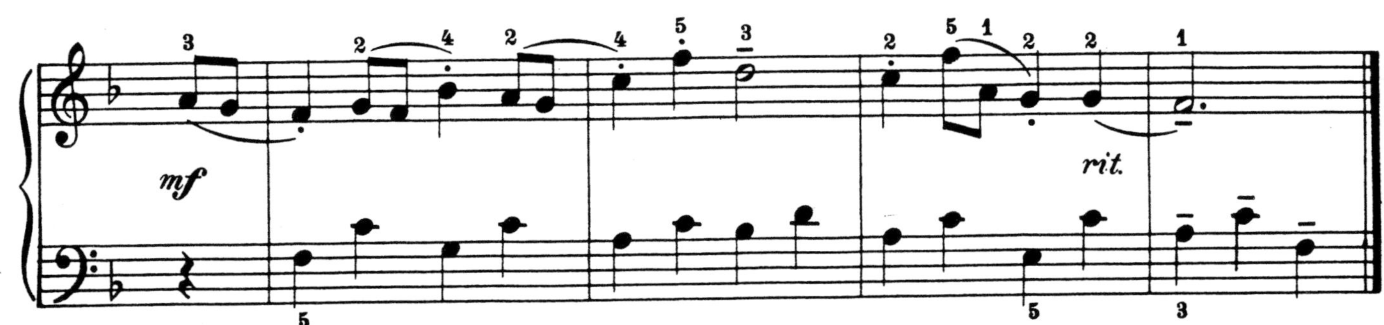

from Piano Album

To Jay Stewart

MEXICAN CHA-CHA-CHA

DAVID CARR GLOVER

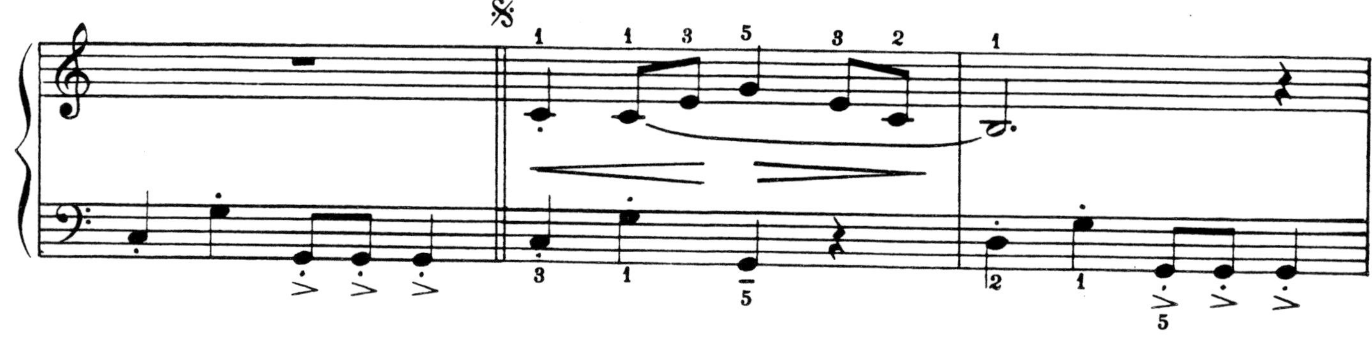

f
mf
mf
f
mf
D. S. al Fine
f

SPOOKY GAMES

DAVID CARR GLOVER

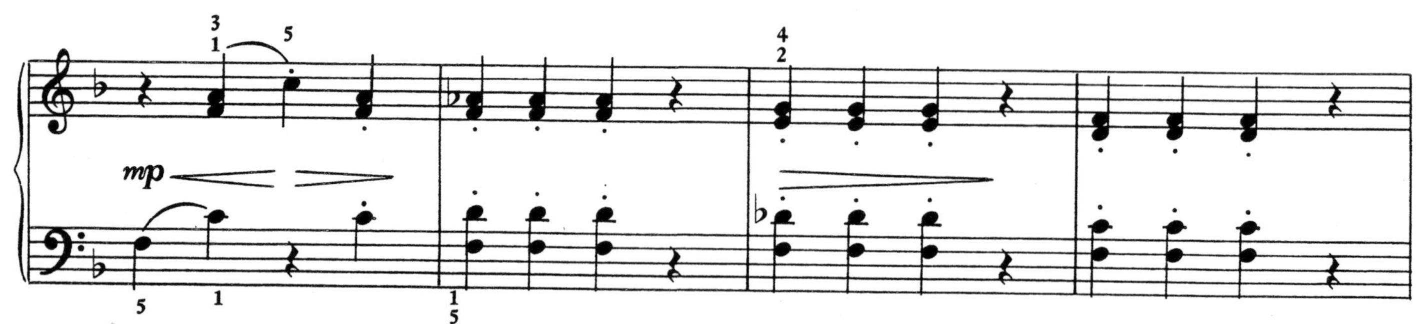

mf
mp
mp
rit.
a tempo
mf
f
mf
mp
ten.
ten.
f
8va
ff
8va

DANCE OF THE MOUNTAIN DWARFS

FRANZ MITTLER

from *Music for Happiness, Book One* (EL02523)

f
r. h.
l. h.
p
dim.

ACROBATICS

With great daring

ROGER GROVE

p
R.H.
L.H.
f
L.H.
R. H.
8va
p
R.H.
L.H.
f
L.H.
mf
R.H.
L.H.
cresc.
8va
L.H.

TANGO BONGO

MARK NEVIN

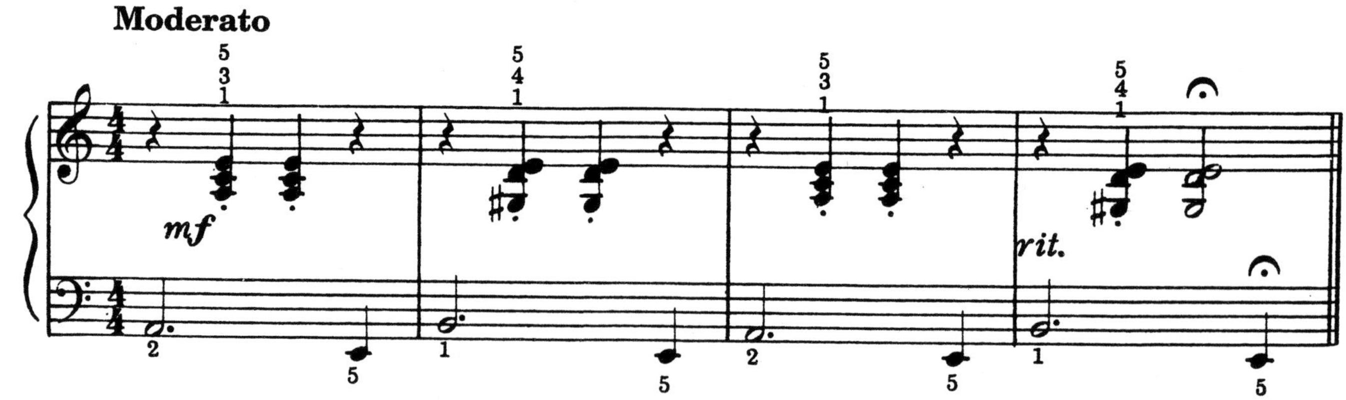

ff
mf

mp
rit.
mf
a tempo
ff

To Kelly Miller

DESERT DANCE

WILLIAM SCHER

f
mp
f
mp
rit.
Slower
mp
rit.

mf
a tempo

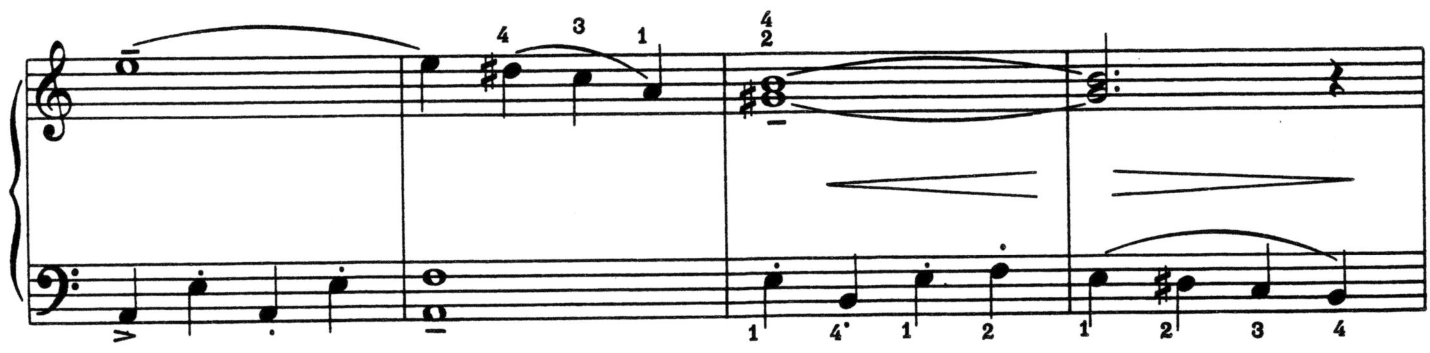

TERESITA

HAZEL COBB

Moderato

mf

f

f

f

8va

loco

f

f

f

8va

loco

Fine

l.h.
l.h.
l.h.
l.h.
f
l.h.
l.h.
l.h.
l.h.
D.C. al Fine

To Susan

I FOUND A STAR

WALTER NOONA

rit. e dim.
mp
ped. simile
Coda
mp
p
8va
r.h.
(l.h. over)
r.h.
l.h.
rit.

BANJO STRUMMER

MARK NEVIN

f
8va
p
mf
8va

DANCING IN MY DREAMS

MARYANNE NAGY

mf
5
1
1
5
1
rit.
Coda
rit.

BROWN BEAR BOOGIE

ALFA KENT

mp
mf
8
8

SUNSET

CARRIE KRAFT

Sunset - 2 - 1

from At Night On The Prairie

l.h.
mf
a tempo
l.h.
l.h.
l.h.
l.h.
r.h.
pp
8va

CHROMATIC HEY-DAY

MARK NEVIN

p
f
ff

TOY SOLDIER BLUES

MARVIN KAHN

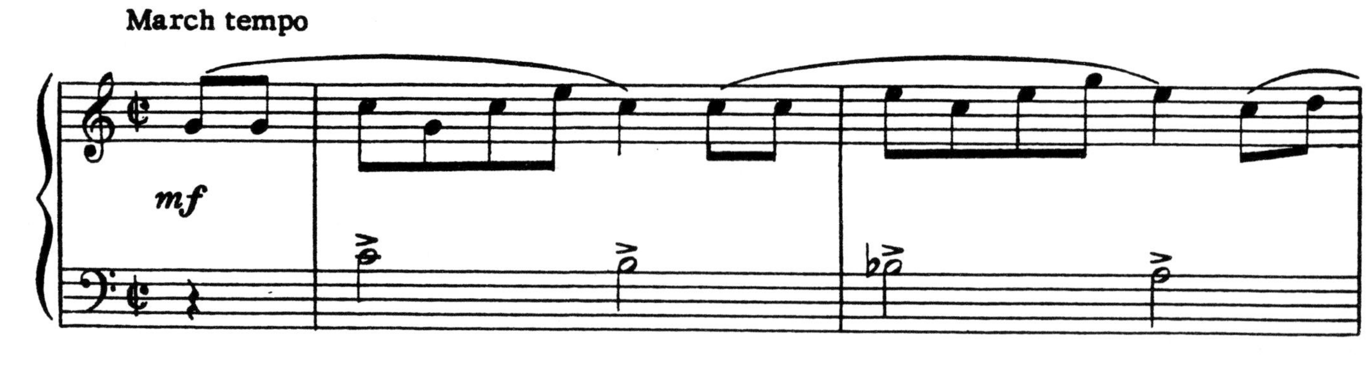

from Piano Moods

Toy Soldier Blues - 2 - 1

f
mf
mp
f
p
mp
f
p
f
f
mf
sfz
ff
mp
r. h.
l. h.

MAY I HAVE THIS WALTZ WITH YOU?

LOUIS SUGARMAN

from *Music for Happiness, Book One*

dim.
Fine
Moderato
mf
D.C. al Fine

ALLEGRO MODERATO

a musical conversation

JON GEORGE

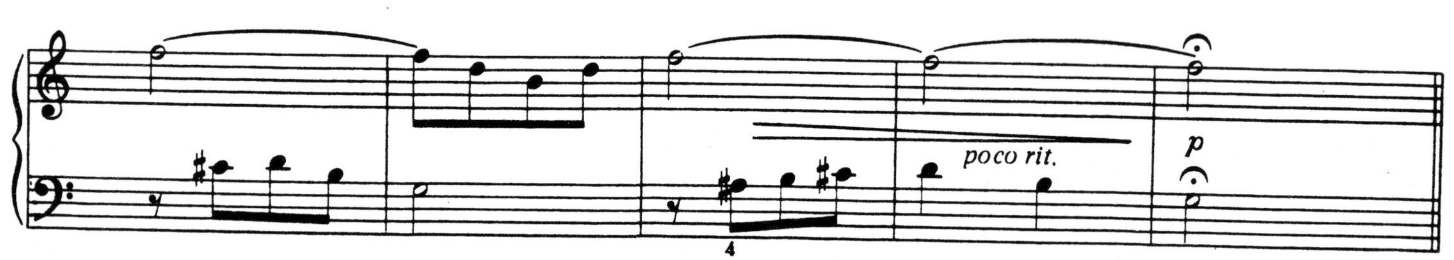

from *Artistry, Repertoire 2*

mf a tempo

poco
a
poco

crescendo
f

MAMBO BOOGIE

Moderately

JOHN W. SCHAUM

5
3
2
4
4
2
3
5
3
2
4
4
2
3
5
5
2
5
2
5
4
5
3
4
2

SPACE HERO

Majestically

JOAN LAST

from The Astronaut

DULCIMER TUNE

JON GEORGE

*These 3 notes are played simultaneously; the "grace note" is then released immediately.

GENTLE GOODBYE

ROGER GROVE

FAVORITE PIANO SOLOS
BLUE RIBBON ENCYCLOPEDIA

Rave reviews keep coming: the "Blue Ribbon" books have indeed been accorded blue ribbon status by teachers and students across the country.

- ✔ Music carefully selected by teacher/editor Carole Flatau
- ✔ Music by composers who specialize in writing for students
- ✔ Music with genuine pedagogical merit
- ✔ Music that reinforces specific concepts and keyboard skills
- ✔ Music of various styles in each volume
- ✔ Music that is good to teach
- ✔ MUSIC THAT STUDENTS REALLY ENJOY!!

LEVEL ONE (EL9792)

Forty titles on 72 pages, including: Beaded Moccasins (B. Frost) • Calypso Tune (J. George) • Daydreams (W. Gillock) • Doo-Dad Boogie (D.C. Glover) • Moon March (E. Pearce) • The Pleasant Peasant (J. George) • Puppet on a String (D. Karp) • Simple Soul (R. Grove) • The Trumpet Player (H. Cobb) • Two Marionettes (J.R. Poe) • Walkin' the Bass (M. Marwick).

LEVEL TWO (EL9793)

Thirty-six selections on 72 pages, including: A la Sonatina (L. Curcio) • Brown Bear Boogie (A. Kent) • Dance of the Mountain Dwarfs (F. Mittler) • The Daring Cossack (W. Noona) • I Found a Star (W. Noona) • Melody for a Monday Morning (R. Steiner) • Stroll on a Warm Day (L.F. Olson) • Sunset (C. Kraft) • Teresita (H. Cobb) • Toy Soldier Blues (M. Kahn).

LEVEL THREE (EL9794)

Thirty-three pieces on 72 pages, including: Coffee Beans (W. Noona) • Give the Bassist a Break (R. Kelley) • Glass Bells (H. Cobb) • The Hunters (D.C. Glover) • Island Song (O.N. Russell) • Jazz Miniatures (M. Nevin) • Miles of Blue (T. Caramia) • Reflections of the Moon (O. Dungan) • Rock 'n' Roll Boogie (J.W. Schaum) • Struttin' (J. Edison).

LEVEL FOUR (EL9795)

Twenty-nine songs on 76 pages, including: Chili-Sauce (H.A. Fischler) • Cool Mule (M. Kahn) • Craggy Gardens in the Spring (S.L. Dittenhaver) • Gypsy Campfire (L. Sugarman) • Jazz Prelude (M. Nevin) • Lotus Flowers in the Wind (W. Scher) • Portrait of Gershwin (G. Bermont) • Reflections in the Rain (W. Noona) • Spanish Blues (M. Kahn) • Winter Wind (G.C. Menotti).

Alfred Publishing Co., Inc.
16320 Roscoe Blvd., Suite 100
P.O. Box 10003
Van Nuys, CA 91410-0003
alfred.com

EL9793 $9.95 in

0 29156 90316 4
ISBN 0-7692-1828-8